貧民窟にて歌ふ

KAGAWA

SONGS FROM THE SLUMS

·

POEMS BY
TOYOHIKO KAGAWA

INTERPRETATION BY
LOIS J. ERICKSON

INTRODUCTION BY
SHERWOOD EDDY

ILLUSTRATIONS BY
JULIAN BRAZELTON

·

COKESBURY PRESS
NASHVILLE, TENNESSEE

SONGS FROM THE SLUMS
COPYRIGHT, MCMXXXV
BY WHITMORE & SMITH

SET UP, PRINTED, AND BOUND BY THE PARTHENON CRAFTSMEN AT NASHVILLE, TENNESSEE, UNITED STATES OF AMERICA

THIS ENGLISH VERSION OF
DR. TOYOHIKO KAGAWA'S POEMS
IS LOVINGLY INSCRIBED

TO

BARNERD AND EDITH
ALEX AND ELINOR

FOREWORD

Toyohiko Kagawa wrote these poems when he was a consumptive boy living in the slums of Japan. Surrounded by hideous things—plague, stench, disease—he sees children kicked naked into the streets; a little girl he loves sold. When put into prison as an agitator, the stars shining through iron bars are his only friends. A tiny one rescued from professional baby-killers and dying in his arms, flutters back to life when she feels his tears upon her face.

Visions come of the things God will do through him. At times despair overwhelms. Tears flow in floods when he fears that human love is shutting him away from God. But there is ecstasy at last when he stands in the sunshine before a little hut, hand in hand with his bride, and

> "Our glad souls fly
> To the scarlet sky,
> Wing to wing;

Ah, the only voice that can call us home
Is the cry of the poor we have left in the
slums!"

L. J. E.

CONTENTS

•

INTRODUCTION

•

WHEN A SUPREMELY SENSITIVE SOUL comes
face to face with the tragedy of life the world
is often permanently richer. This was true
when the young prince, Gautama, who had
long been carefully secluded from even a
glimpse of the harsh side of human existence,
received his vision of suffering as he beheld
examples of old age, sickness, and death.
It was true when the Troubador of Christ in
Assisi turned from the revelings of his gay
comrades to kiss the tainted flesh of a leper
in the way.

The contents of this book reveal that it has
occurred once more, as a young man in Japan,
who has the delicacy of perception for which
his race is known, and the ability of its
artists to sound the depths of life with a few
deft strokes of the brush or a poem of seventeen syllables, comes face to face with the in-
justice and tragedy that are bred in our
present industrial system. In these poems
Kagawa brings us alternately into the joyous

presence of Beauty in the open face of Nature, and then the ghastly reality of the hell on earth that man's inhumanity to man has made. The one relieves the other. With Kagawa's faith and love we are able constantly to lift our eyes above the sordid slums of man to the shining stars of God.

These poems do not seem so much to seize upon the instances of pathos and beauty which the author has known in his unique career, and to set them before us, as they seize us and plunge us into his life, until we share his wonder at the mystery and loveliness of nature, and partake of his passion of rebellion at needless human squalor and cruelty. It is the youthful Kagawa who writes these poems, haunted as he is by the vision of what must be achieved when God works through his hand, and overwhelmed with the poignant tragedy of modern industrialism which his explorations in the dark, neglected side of a great city's life have revealed.

In these songs there is revealed that master power of sensing the sacramental significance of common things. They are not mere lumps of matter for him but they are vibrant with the purposes of God. He finds the ecstasy of the springtime that is denied a dweller in the slums compared in the blossom of a

single flower growing in the mire; he forgets
the prison chains as he gazes from the window
of his cell on a starlit night.

Kagawa has written:

"Do you hear God's pain-pitched cry as
He suffers because of the world's sore dis-
tress? Yes, I hear it! I hear it! I feel within
me the beating pulse of the universe. I hear
the deep sighings of God."

Like many noble and gentle souls who have
preceeded him, he has been able to "find the
Christ through tears." His Bible is not a
mere book, but the pulsing life that passes
beneath his window in the slums. His
Christ, and the Christ of these poems, is one
who goes to his death anew in the person of
the victims of leprosy and tuberculosis who
knows the dull despair of the unemployed,
and is no stranger to the crushing woe of the
women sold into the captivity of lust that
they and their families may eat bread.

The reading of the songs in this book
will bring tears to the eyes of many—a
tribute to the artistic balance of its realism
as well as to the pathos and beauty of the
human picture it portrays.

The forces that have made a waste of the
world today are common to the Shinkawa
of Kobe, the East Side of New York, and
London's Bow. Kagawa is not confronting

us with some far-off tragedy of another hemisphere, but one in which our own hands are red with guilt. Perhaps this, in addition to being the terrific indictment of the picture which the book gives, is also its chief message of hope. Its author, as we know, dreams of a fellowship of Christians around the earth, of a Christian Internationale, whose members, sustaining and supporting each other, shall launch a common attack upon the social sin which embodies itself in a system whose chief by-product is debauched, debased, and prostituted human lives.

If the challenge of Kobe's slums is not peculiar to Japan, but is common to the East and the West, may it not be the means of bringing forth a new, militant solidarity among those whose privilege it is to make up the body of Christ on earth?

"Fervent the vow I swore to fight, nor falter;
Fight with a faith not flickering, nor dim;
God is my Father; in my heart an altar
Glows with the sacrifice I offer Him."

SHERWOOD EDDY.

New York, N. Y.
October, 28, 1935.

新 川

SHINKAWA

●

One month in the slums,
And I am sad,
So sad
I seem devil-possessed,
Or mad.

Sweet Heaven sends
No miracle
To ease
This hell;
The careless earth
Rings no
Alarum bell.

But here there are slippery streets, which
never are dry;
They are lined with open sewers, where rats
come out to die;
Tattered paper doors stand wide to winds
that beat;
The houses are all of a reddish black, like the
hue of stale whale meat;

Filth on the flimsy ceilings, dirt in the musty
       air;
Elbowed out of their crowded rooms, people
       are everywhere;
All night long they crouch in the cold,
       huddled on broken benches,
Where there's never a moment's lifting of
       the heavy offal stenches.

    The painted idiot girl,
        Upon whose back
        Vile pictures
        Were tattooed
            In red,
  Will never lure men to her den again;
        She is dead. . . . .

        You ordinary folk
        Upon the hill,
            To whom
        The slums are vague,
        Listen and tremble
        As I scream to you,
        "SHE DIED OF PLAGUE!"

        I came to bring
        God to the slum;
        But I am dumb,
           Dismayed;

Betrayed
By those
Whom I would aid;
Pressed down,
So sad
I fear
That I am mad.

Pictures
Race through my brain
And lie
Upon my heart.
Pictures like this:
A man,
Legs rotted off
With syphilis;
And yet,
He need not fret
That money
Does not come,
Because his wife
Is rented out
And brings
Sufficient sum. . . . .

I hear
A harsh voice
Cry out,
"Here you! Dance!"
I see a thin child dodge

And I know
It is the boy
Whose father
              Kicks him.
Twelve years old,
Driven from bed
Into the streets,
Naked and cold. . . . .

I must be done with thoughts like these!

The raindrops patter slowly from the eaves;
The fire beneath my half-boiled rice is out;
I hear the rising roar of ribald shout
That brings the evening to Shinkawa Slum.

Is there no way
That help can come?

春夜

SPRING NIGHT

●

One sweet spring night,
Two little actress girls,
Dressed all in red,
Their faces powdered
To a ghastly white,
Sat in the doorway
Of a restaurant
Blazing with lights;
There they played
The koto.

As they sang,
The music
Trickled
Like a little brook
Out of a valley,
While their voices rose,
Piercing and clear,
Or died
In whispers.

Crowds
Stood there
And stared,
And stared;
And I stared
With them.

Then I went away
And hid my face,
And wept—
Wept for the woe
Those little singing girls
Must know!

たゞ一輪の花

ONLY A FLOWER

●

Strange that the spring has come
On meadow and vale and hill,
For here in the sunless slum
My bosom is frozen still.
And I wear the wadded things
Of the dreary winter days,
But out of the heart of this
       little flower
God gazes into my face!

山楊の國

THE LAND OF HAN

●

"He cannot save
    Himself"—
    Long ago,
The crowds
Reviled a Man
    Who came
To save them.
And I,
Who fain would follow Him,
    Am spent.
For I can see
    No hope
For the slums,
Because that,
First of all,
This thing
Is wrong—
That men
Should crowd
Thus in the dearth
And dark,
And dirt—
Should crowd and throng.

I would lead them away from their bondage,
 on, and on, and on,
To the North Land, the Land of Trees, the
 lovely Land of Han;
Where mosquitoes never torture, and there's
 never pain to bear,
But flower buds are bursting, and spring is
 everywhere;
Where fairy fragrance flutters on the clean,
 cool breeze,
And tiny, straw-thatched home-huts are nes-
 tled 'neath the trees;
Where bonny birds sing gaily in the glory of
 the dawn,
And friendly folk fare forth to work each
 bright and happy morn;
Where the sun shines out in splendor when the
 white mist fades,
Where the crystal streamlets tinkle, and there
 comes the twinkle, twinkle,
Of the sunlight falling, flashing on the spades.
Where the hazy purple mountains and the
 blue, blue rivers sing,
"God is here around you! He is here in
 everything!"
Yes; I would lead my people on, and on, and
 on,
To the North Land, the Land of Trees, the
 lovely Land of Han!

But oh, in my heart there is pity,
For my people must stay in the city,
And this six-foot shack that shelters me
Is the only place where I want to be.

貧民窟の宵

SLUM EVENING

●

I walk the bright, hot streets,
And suddenly the sunshine shows
     How soiled my sleeve is.

    When the evening comes,
      Tired, oh, so tired,
      I wander home
      To an empty house;
        Lonely,
        Cheerless,
        Fireless,
        Doorless;
    No one to greet me here.

      And so,
     I drop down
     On the sill
    To watch the sunset.

    My sick neighbor there,
The one whose head is stiff upon his neck,
    Boils me some gruel,

And comes bringing it.

I watch men thronging home,
    No work to do,
They idle all day long,
    Day after day.
    Slowly the sun goes down.

Rice gruel and dried plums,
The gruel thin and white,
The plums blood-red.

    I eat;
    Night falls
    I throw myself
    Down on my bed. . . . .

我が弟子達

MY DISCIPLES

●

Three disciples have I,
Three, or four.
Little shaven-headed,
Dirty-nosed
Tako
And loud-voiced
Jinko,
Who will not lose me from their sight,
Are numbers One and Two.

The Beggar's Chief
Is Number Three.
He did not know
How to bow
At the Christmas feast,
And so,
He turned swift somersaults.

The Fourth
Is Baby Dekobo.
He cannot lisp
His father's name,

But all the day,
He calls,
"Ten-tei! Ten-tei!"

So lovely,
Twelve years old, and sold. . . . .
For hours she cried outside my door
Because she had to go.
The little girl who loves me most
Is Kiyo-ko.

星だにあらば

IF ONLY THERE ARE STARS

●

If only there are stars,
  I have my friends.
  But in the dark
I think upon my fate,
    And all
  My spirit sickens
And the hard tears fall.

  Around my prison
Runs a high stockade;
  And from my wrists
    Chains dangle;
    But no power
  Can lock my eyes.

  So can I steal
  This lovely light
    That wraps me—
    This radiance
    That drips
  Out of the Dipper.

Dragging my chains
    I climb
To the tall window-ledge;
    And though
My body cannot crawl
Between those grim iron rods,
    Still can I
Laugh as my spirit flies
Into the purple skies!

Northward and northward,
    Up and up,
Up to the world of light
    I go bounding;
Farewell, O Earth, farewell,
What need I now of your freedom?

Fearless, I fly and fly,
On through the heavenly sky;
Breaking all prison bars,
My soul sleeps with the stars!

雪 の 朝

SNOWY MORNING

●

Six in the morning;
　　It is dark
　　And cold.
A little figure
Stands by the sake shop,
Her head bowed down
Against an empty cart.

She wears the rags
　　She slept in.
　　Her mother
　　Has pawned
　　Her clothes;
And as she starts
　　For the factory,
　　Foodless,
　　She has come
　　So far,
　　And stopped. . . . .

　　It is Yoshiko
Shamed, and hungry, and cold,
　　Crying in the snow.

相共に泣く時

WHEN TEARS ARE MINGLED

●

Dawn coming in through the greyness
Lights up the place where she lies;
I am sodden with sleep, but I waken
At my starveling's fretful cries.

She is here on the floor beside me
Wrapped in rags that stink;
I change them;
I hold her to feed her,
And sob as she struggles to drink.

Three days have I now been a woman,
With a mother's heart in my breast;
Do I doze but an hour
Then she whimpers,
And I spring to soothe her to rest.

Thin little dirty baby,
Wailing with pain all the while,
But I taste the bliss that no life should miss
When I look in her eyes and smile!

Ah, she is ill
Little Ishi,
Life has abused her so;
Safe from the fiend who had meant to kill,
Fever has laid her low.

Through the night I labored to save her;
We two were all alone.
Sharp in the fearful stillness
The neighbor's clock struck one.

Then walls went creaking, creaking,
Blackened timbers groaned.
In this house by murder haunted,
The low-hung ceilings moaned.

Boards in the floor beneath us
Which have sucked blood, warm and bright,
Held their breath and shrieked of death
Into the ghostly night. . . . .

Why is the world so cruel?
Seen with Ishi's eyes,
The earth, and all things in it,
Is a mountain-pile of ice.

Then do you pity Ishi?
I need your pity, too.
I must help; I must help,
But am helpless.

Oh, to be taught what to do!
Men are consoled by their women,
But this scrap in my tired arm lies,
A shriveled doll from the junk-heap,
And the strong man who holds her cries.

Why are you quiet, Ishi?
Why are your eyes shut, why?
Wait, oh wait, little sick one,
It is too soon to die.
Think of my struggle to save you,
Will you not stay with me?
Listen; Death shall not take you;
I have no burial fee!

(How now?
Through the daze of this dreadful plight
Do I wince at a bedbug's filthy bite?)

Cry again, little Ishi;
Cry once more, once more;
What will it take to make you wake?
For I cannot let you go!

I call; but you do not hear me;
I clasp you; you do not move.
It is not to pain I would bring you again,
There is Love in the world; there is Love!

Will she not cry?
   I shall make her;
   Here in my close embrace
I kiss her wan lips growing greyer;
My drawn face touches her face.
Fast are my frightened tears flowing,
   Falling on Ishi's eyes;
With her cold, still tears they are mingled,
O God . . . . at last . . . . she cries!

猿まはし

MONKEY-BOY

●

Today I saw a monkey-boy
Standing before a toy-shop,
Gazing with all his eyes
Down at the toys.
His face was red and round,
Not quite an idiot face;
Sixteen or seventeen he was,
A bumpkin in tight trousers,
Leggings, and sandals
Made of straw.

Upon his back
Was strapped a bundle
Wrapped in black,
On which a monkey sat.

Monkey and master,
Both alike,
Gazed on the toys,
Motionless.

I marveled

At their tirelessness,
And borrowing
Their unconcern,
I stopped
And gazed
At them,
And gazed.

One minute passed;
Two minutes . . . .
Three . . . .
And neither moved.
They had not even blinked.

Four minutes . . . .
Five . . . .
And still
They had not looked their fill.

What were they thinking
As they watched
The strange springs move?
What does the fever
Of existence
Mean
To creatures
Such as these?

O Monkey-Boy,
I, too,
Want a toy!

DREAMS

●

Day after day,
I fight
With all my might.
And when night comes
I ease my bony body down
Into a yellow chair
In our small church.

And there,
The while
My heart is full
Of praise and prayer,
The leader's voice
Fades slowly,
Slowly,
Slowly,
Into air.

I jerk
Myself
Awake;
My eyes stretch wide,

And fill with tears,
Remembering my sin.
And then,
I feel again
The comfort of forgiveness.

But in a little while,
I nod,
And nod,
And nod,
Falling . . . .
Falling . . . .
Into the gleams
That light my path of dreams.

Half-waking, and half-sleeping,
Visions around me creeping;
Even as dusk is neither day nor night,
So fancy is weaving, weaving,
A web for my soul's believing,
And God is one with my dream—
He is one with my dream of delight.

Ah, little heart, as you nod,
How happy these visions of God!

我窗外

OUTSIDE MY WINDOW

●

Outside my window
Noisy voices rise
Shouting my name;
And I,
(Would-be philosopher,
Apostle thinly clad),
Within my den
Raise up my head,
And look to see
Who calls.

Is it a human mother
Suckling there
Her clock-faced boy
With filthy nose.
Or are they animals
Far, far removed from man?
The glass distorts them. . . . .
There a little girl
Frolics about,
Face painted
With a fierce moustache . . . .

A baby toddles by . . . .
The bell upon a dog's neck
      Tinkles. . . . .
Tiny new-hatched
Chickens cheep. . . . .

Cast-off clogs,
And broken sandals,
And foul, reeking mud
Make one great compost-heap . . . .
      Everywhere
I know that vile things
Jump, and crawl, and leap. . . . . .

     Chatter, chatter;
     Peep, peep;
     Clatter, clatter;
     Mumble, tumble;
     Grumble, rumble;
     Growl, yowl, howl. . . . .

     And over all
     The hot rays
     Of the sun
     Beat on the slum
     Like some
     Great drum. . . . .

This is no time
  Nor place
For cold philosophy.

Come, little black-nosed babe,
Come fierce moustache,
  Come dog,
Come dirty chicks,
We shall join hands,
  And prance,
  And dance,
  And dance. . . . .

復讐

REVENGE

•

If I could search the deepest depths of space,
Or if these eyes of flesh could scan what lies
      beyond the utmost bound of heaven,
Still could I not perceive the form of God.

And yet, would it be well to swallow up this
      Space—
To grasp Love and Desire and all Reality,
As though the Universe were but a grain of
      sand,
And swallowing,
Should seek to see if this would choke me?

In with thee, Space!
Thou art as light to gulp as is the air,
Thou meaningless, shapeless, worthless, life-
      less thing of cast-off skin!

    Out! Out! Out!
    Out from my lungs! Out!
    I spew thee out again!

And now afar,
Behold again
A star . . . . a star . . . .
Here Mars . . . . there Hercules. . . . .

No; Space is heavy, grave. It weeps not; loves
       not; has no sweet, soft lips.
Oh, God,
This that I vomit forth is blood, and quivering
       flesh—
Ephemeral!

Now, who can quench the sun?
Since Space is ugly, quench it. Go!
Quench that great wealth of light,
That brilliancy which dazzles.

Quench it;
Blow
With all your strength;
And it will wink out,
Thus. . . . .

      So shall I be revenged
      Because I cannot make
      Vile things, and sad,
      Glad things, and beautiful!

秋 の 日向

AUTUMN SUNSHINE

•

O golden autumn sun,
    You are a comet,
    Rushing, whirling
    Through the sky!
Down at the wretched slum
    I live in
You gild the sooty sills
    As you pass by.

You have made me happy, happy, happy;
You shone into my dingy little room
On the penny-posy in my gargle-bottle,
And the little bud has broken into bloom!

地球も月の如くに

THE EARTH GROWN LIKE THE MOON
A Vision

•

The earth
Is like the moon,
Cold crystal,
Flowers of ice.
It is a desert,
Skyless,
Lifeless;
For mankind
Has laid it waste.

The earth is frozen,
Glittering like a jewel,
Yet
Ruined by pride.

Seen from a star,
The earth gleams
Like the moon.
Mount Fuji glistens,
And the Alps
Glow in their glory.

Jerusalem,
Tokyo,
The slums of London,
And the underworld
Of Paris—
All are shadows.

Living things
Have left the earth
Forsaken.
They rebel
At dwelling
In its ugliness.
Still the world
Whirls on,
In agony.

Lo, man's sin
Is great
Before his God;
His world
A waste.

Graves of heroes
And of harlots
Both alike
Are dust,
And dust alone.

God has at length
Frozen the world
Cold as the moon.

(And why should not God's love for us
grow dim,
This world which has no love or use for Him?)

木蓮

MOKUREN

●

Above the temple wall
Great waxen blossoms bloom;
Gleaming boughs alight with white
Against the gloom.
Beautiful,
From morn till even
Up, up they climb,
Trying to peep at Heaven.
Flowers alone,
Green leaves not yet unfurled—
The only lovely, flaunting things
In all the chill, drab world.

The earth and I are drab and tired,
But very, very soon
We shall be mad with beauty
When the fairy cherries bloom!

The *mokuren* blossoms are much like magnolias, but the flowers
come on the bare branches before the leaves are out.

月光輝やく

THE MOON LOOKS DOWN

•

A drunken man
Was going through a soldiers' drill
Outside my door.

"About Face! Forward March!"
He called.
The alley echoed
To his fierce commands
And trembled to his tread.

Suddenly
I sprang before him,
Mimicking his words,
"About Face! Forward March!
Repent, and turn to good!"

But I was frightened
At my own loud voice,
And as I lit my lamp,
My knees began to shake
Because I thought,

"What if he comes
To stab me with a knife?"

But no;
He entered, saying,
"Yes; your words are good.
Yet, as for me,
The God of Heaven
Has cast me off.
And how shall I believe
That He will save?
But say
That you will save me.
For I know
That you are in the slum
To save the poor who come."

Troubled,
There I sat
Upon my pallet.
What to say to him
To move his heart?
At last came words of love.

Silently he sat and listened.
After me,
My helper-friend,
Hasukajima,
Word by word,
Slowly word by word,
Showed him our Lord.

Then
The drunken man
Burst into weeping
As he told his tale.

When he was two weeks old
His mother cast him
Out on the sea-beach,
There to die—
He cursed her for a harlot,
Bitterly.

When he was grown
To fifteen years,
He drew a sword
Upon a man,
Demanding money;
And to hide a theft,
Burned down a home.
Nine years he was in jail.
He shook with sobbing,
As he told his tale—
A vagabond,
The sad slum's masterpiece.

And as we heard his sins,
We wept with him;
Wildly he wrung his hands,
And rent his clothes
In grief,
As he implored
Forgiveness.

Softly,
We soothed his fears,
Knowing we find
The Christ
Through tears.

I prayed;
Then Tora said,
"Tonight I sleep with you!"
I threw my door ajar,
And looked
Up at the winter moon—

And even there, in that clear, cloudless sky,
I could not see the beauty passing by,
The moon itself seemed drunken,
            weeping, lost. . . . .

Hasukajima
Knelt with me
  Down in the dust
  To pray.

The clocks strike midnight.

Far away,
The moon looks down
Upon the slums,
Touching the little homes,
One by one,
One by one.

Still sobbing,
Tora comes,
Naked,
And runs
To turn
A strong, cold stream
Of water
On his body,
Sobering himself
From *sake*.

The moon peeps through the tattered door,
Silvering the filthy walls,
Watching us sleeping on the broken floor.

火鉢に凭りて

BESIDE MY BRAZIER

●

Unloved and lonely
Here I sit
Leaning against
My brazier;
Now and then
I raise myself
To rake dead ashes.

Listlessly,
I look about the room.
Newspapers
Pasted on the walls
Show pictures
Of a worthless world.

I cannot sing,
For doctors
Have forbidden it.
They cannot forbid
My prayers.

I have forsworn
Learning and love.
Lonely I
Sit, and
Only cry . . . .
And weep . . . .
And sob. . . . .

O devil-world,
I pile
Tears upon tears
Till I am spent,
But not,
Not yet,
Will you repent.

God,
How I long for Thee!
All feeling else is gone.
This three-mat hole
Where sunlight never strikes,
This poverty so dread
That I would fain
Cast out the cat
I cannot feed,
(The cat that comes
Again, and yet again)—

But I am satisfied,
Satisfied. . . . .

My eyes behold Thee here,
And when I close them
I
Can feel Thee watching
By my side.

Farewell to paper-pasted walls;
I get me up
And shove my shoddy sandals on.

Throughout this land
I go to preach,
"The Kingdom is at hand!"

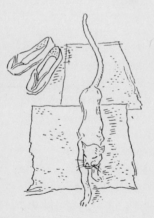

失業

JOBLESS

●

Crunching the frost
A figure hurries down the street,
Buffeted by
The cold, keen wind;
And as he passes on,
He always seeks the sunny side
To walk along.

He throws himself
Down in a bright, warm spot
Beside a bank—
One of the jobless throng
That haunt the city.
Men go rushing past;
The tide of traffic roars.
But by and by,
All huddled in a heap,
He falls asleep.

Hour after hour
He dozes . . . . wakes . . . .
And dozes . . . .

And the bean-curd seller
Passes by.

The sleeper rouses up,
Hearing the tinkling bell,
Eager to snatch it,
Impetuous
To find a way
Out of his hell
Of bitter idleness—
Alas! He has no bell!

He flings himself
Against the wind,
Ashamed to sleep and doze.

"O sun,"
He thinks,
"Are you as lone as I,
Up in your empty sky?"

Feeling,
"Ah, the sun,
The sun,
Is my fast friend.
I love him;
He loves me;
He loves me,
And he gives
This sweet and pleasant warmth.

But he is far,
So far,
Away.
I cannot touch
Nor thank him,
And my heart is sad.

As for the world,
It is too wide,
Too wide and cold."

"Ji-RIN! Ji-RIN!"
A bell comes jingling down the
      street,
A loud voice calling,
"To-o-o-fu! To-o-o-fu!"

泥濘

MUD

●

The leather tips
Of my high clogs
Are gone.
And so I stumble
As I feel my way
Along the muddy paths.
The streets
Are sloughs of slime
After the rain—
Rutted with wheel-tracks;
Ploughed with wooden shoes;
Strewn with the skins
Of oranges;
Blood-red
With scattered bits
Of paper handbills.

Through the mire
Wade ragged boys and girls.
Yonder I see
A fool go past,
His silly mouth

Wide open.
There a wet policeman stands;
A rickshaw splashes by.
The muddy pools
Mirror the wretched shops.

Clop, clop,
My clogs
Go stumbling
Through the slop.

上衣一枚きり

ONE GARMENT LEFT

•

I have no one
To make a garment
For me;
Nor yet
A garment to be made.
My clothes
Are soiled,
And torn,
And tattered.
On the streets,
The people stare at me
Each time I leave the slums.

But those who clothe themselves
In borrowed garb
Are like a crow
Wearing a peacock's feathers—
Fools!

As for myself,
Bare legs,
Short shirt,

Sweatband on brow,
I gird me up
To move the world!

And when
I wash
My one poor garment,
Stiff with filth,
Naked,
I wait
For it to dry.

Naked,
I kneel
Down at the crossing
In the mud,
To weep
And pray.

Stripped thus of all that Thou hast given me,
Lord, I would give again my all to Thee!

妹

LITTLE SISTER

•

She leaves her bed
At five;
And it is ten
At night
When she comes home again.

She has her bath,
And does her hair;
And then
'Tis almost midnight
When she kneels to pray
After her heavy day.

Often beside
The whirring wheels
Her head droops down,
Half-starved for sleep. . . . .

My little sister
Of the factory
Is sweet.

發見

DISCOVERY

●

I cannot invent
New things,
Like the airships
Which sail
On silver wings;
But today
A wonderful thought
In the dawn was given,
And the stripes on my robe,
Shining from wear,
Were suddenly fair,
Bright with a light
Falling from Heaven—
Gold, and silver, and bronze
Lights from the windows of Heaven.

And the thought
Was this:
That a secret plan
Is hid in my hand;
That my hand is big,

Big,
Because of this plan.

That God,
Who dwells in my hand,
Knows this secret plan
Of the things He will do for the world
Using my hand!

祈

PRAYER

●

In the clear morning
I have climbed the hill.

Smoke from the factories
Rolls west to east
Across the huge red sun.

A train puffs past
Through tiny, far-off fields.

Bright buds are everywhere.
    God of the hills,
    The smoke,
    The sun,
    The growing grain,
I cannot word my prayer.

God . . . . green things . . . .
Green things . . . . God . . . .
Lord of each little leaf
    On every tree;

Lord of the clouds that drift
    Far out to sea,
    I thank Thee
That Thou has shown
    Jesus
    To me.

    God,
    I pray
    That Thou wilt take
    Evil away.
            AMEN.

無一文

PENNILESS

•

Penniless . . . .
A while
Without food
I can live;
But it breaks my heart
To know
I cannot give.

Penniless . . . .
I can share my rags,
But I—
I cannot bear to hear
Starved children cry.

Penniless . . . .
And rain falls,
But trust is true.
Helpless, I wait to see
What God will do.

斯の如き者のものなり

"OF SUCH"

●

I would be always but a little child,
Stretching my eager fingers out to catch
   the rain;
To touch the bright, sweet flowers;
         On the path I pass
To hear the noisy insects in the grass.
         Always would I know
The thrilling wonder of my first white snow!

I would be always innocent:
         Would always learn;
Would greet each dawn with glee;
Ah, it is much, is much,
To know the Coming Kingdom is of such!

日暮

DAY'S END

●

Day ends:
Breasting the North,
My shoulders shiver
As I onward go.
And yet,
I utterly forget
The cruel cold,
Nor feel the dark,
Because my heart
Aches with the people's woe.

Oh, let me trust
That through my tears
God's Kingdom has
One little inch drawn near!
Then what is it to me
That my weak body be
Beaten to dust?
Midnight:
I crawl from out my bed
Into the cold,

And gaze up at the stars again,
Finding God there
To help me bear
My daily load
Of grief and care,
Sorrow and pain.

Deep in the night
Our spirits meet,
And prayer is sweet!

幽靈的存在

A WRAITH'S EXISTENCE

●

The things
I get of life
Grow daily less.
Pale-faced,
I eat coarse rice;
My bloodless body
Shivers.

I have no house,
And so
The library
At school
Becomes my home,
And there I pass my time.

They say that spring
Has come;
But no flowers bloom,
And I must still breathe on
The cold raw air
Of winter.
But my frozen flesh,

Dissolving,
Leaves me limbless—
Only a thin, grey ghost . . . .

O spring-time sun,
Look down
And shed a tear
For this poor wraith,
For me!

霊 の 彫 刻 師

SCULPTOR OF THE SOUL

•

I fain would be a sculptor of the soul,
Making each strong line fine,
    Each feature faultless.
    Yet the sculptor cannot carve
    In wood or stone
    An image nobler than he sees
    Within his own stout soul.

So, gazing at the tools within my hand,
I shudder! How escape from self—
    Pitiable, limited—
    That I may be indeed
    God's carver?

Happy is this thought;
There is a Guide for me,
Who in His living flesh
Has given me the perfect image that I
    seek, of God!

我が十字架

MY CROSS

●

The fault is mine;
I cannot pray
In this dark place.
But when I raise my eyes
The form of my
Own formless God
　　　　Is here,
　　　　And I
Can look unto His face.

Accursed,
The green leaves wither;
Swarming flies
Buzz in the wan sunset;
And little, hungry children
By shop doors
Listless, are playing yet.

O God's fair Country!
Bitter Hell!
O present world
Of grief, and pain, and loss!

Their will to live,
Though life be cursed,
That is my cross!

波は静かに

THE WAVES ARE SILENT

●

The waves are silent,
    Men are gone;
Far in the west
    I see the smiling sea,
The sky, the sun
    Melt into mist.

The little glimmering lamps
    In homes where good wives wait,
And flaring torches of the fisher-folk
    Upon the sea,
Pierce through the chill, wet gloom and light
    The loneliness for me.

I muse upon this solitary isle;
    Upon the world;
    The past comes back before me,
        And God's grace;—
    And oh, the sleeve is wet with tears
        That hides my face!

I yearn because my heart is yet
    Far, far from LOVE . . . .
Above me shines the misty moon,
    And no waves move.

愛して呉れるな

LOVE ME NOT

●

Love, linger not to whisper your temptation;
Seek not to bind me with your heavy chain;
I would be free to seek the world's salvation;
I would be free to rescue men from pain.

High is the wall that guards my heart from
          coldness;
Big is the barrier to shut me out from sin;
O Human Love, aflame with passion's bold-
          ness,
Storm not this citadel to enter in.

Fervent the vow I swore to fight, nor falter;
Fight with a faith not flickering, nor dim;
God is my Father; in my heart an altar
Glows with the sacrifice I offer Him.

      Leave me alone, Love,
      Leave my heart alone!

流れよ涙！

FLOW, TEARS!

•

Flow, O my tears!
Well up and fall,
O flood!
Soul of my inmost soul,
Dissolve in grief—
For I have lost
The precious ALL
I offered God.

O tears,
Lift up your doleful voice;
For from the day
I turned to human love,
Forgetting God,
His presence has
Departed from me—
And I know not where!

Lift up your voice,
And scream,
And cry aloud;
Fall tears,

That I may wring you dry.
For I would see my God,
Or failing,
Would
Immerse the world in woe,
Then fling my life away!

Oh, that my tears
Might overflow
The path by which
God flees from me!
Tears of my heart,
Quick! Quick!
Help me to capture Him!

Oh, agony and pain
To long . . . . to long . . . .
To see
The face of God again!

愛

LOVE

●

My God is Love;
My God is Love,
Tender and deep;
I feel His close, sweet presence
Looking down to see
The beggar-baby
Lying in my arms asleep.

新婚

NEW-WEDDED

·

Bright sunshine
On a hut—
Our little hut—
Where we stand,
My love and I,
Heart to heart,
Hand in hand.

As the springtime buds
Grow, close together,
So shall we grow,
Forever and ever.

By the sea
We stand,
My love and I,
Hand in hand;
And our glad souls fly
To the scarlet sky,
Wing to wing—
And the only voice that can call us home
Is the cry of the poor we have left in the slum!

Soon
We may be beaten
By the world;
Flesh fallen away,
Bones broken,
Blood flowing;
Yet shall our spirit lives
Point upward,
Glowing!

O brave one,
And tender,
God-given,
Surely our happiness
Is like Heaven!

Tired of the world,
We can always fly
Up to the wide and wonderful sky,
You and I,
Hand in hand,
Heart to heart,
Wing to wing,
Bright as the rising sun
In spring!

最愛なる者へ

IN THE HEART OF MY HEART

●

You who dwell
In the heart of my heart,
Listen to me;

This you must know—
I am a child of grief and pain,
Bending my fingers to count my woe.

You yield me
Everything;
But I
Have nothing
I can bring
To give to you.

Know
You have married
Poverty, sorrow;
Bear it with me;
The storm will be over
Tomorrow.

A little while
For us
The rod;
And then,
Then, God!

O angel one,
You must not weep;
Come here,
My dear,
Come near. . . . .

重荷

THE BURDEN

●

Take Thou the burden, Lord;
I am exhausted with this heavy load.
My tired hands tremble,
And I stumble, stumble
Along the way.
Oh, lead with Thine unfailing arm
Again today.

Unless Thou lead me, Lord,
The road I journey on is all too hard.
Through trust in Thee alone
Can I go on.

Yet not for self alone
Thus do I groan;
My people's sorrows are the load I bear.
Lord, hear my prayer—
May Thy strong hand
Strike off all chains
That load my well-loved land.
God, draw her close to Thee!

BIOGRAPHICAL

●

TOYOHIKO KAGAWA was born in Kobe, Japan, July
10, 1888. His father was first head of some nineteen
villages in his native province of Awa, and later was
elevated to secretaryship of the Privy Council which,
because of its function of advising the Emperor, was
the most influential body in the Empire. Kagawa's
childhood was a sad one, for he was the son of one of
his father's concubines, and both parents died when he
was four years old. He went to live in the ancestral
village of Awa, in the care of his father's neglected
wife and a foster grandmother. Here, in a great
thatch-roofed farmhouse, he lived a lonely life, abused
and humiliated because of his birth by the two women
in whose care he was placed. Nature was even at
that time the great solace of his heart.

Except for a profligate brother who went through
the family estate in the process of his dissipation, but
whose occasional visits home were a bright spot in
the life of the boy, he knew little real affection until
he entered school in the city of Tokushima. At a
time when he was in danger of succumbing to the
melancholia that often threatens the reserved and
highly sensitive youth of Japan in adolescence, love
came into his life in the person of two missionaries,
Dr. H. W. Myers and Dr. C. A. Logan. Both were
friends and counselors to the lonely lad, and it was
through them that he came to know the personality

of Christ, and to find purpose and meaning in life. With the heart-felt prayer, "O God, make me like Christ," he entered upon that fellowship with God to the reality of which his whole subsequent life has been a testimony.

Reading of the work of Canon Barnett in the slums of London, he decided to dedicate his life to the service of the poor. This choice of religion and vocation brought down the wrath of his uncle, the head of the family, upon him, and resulted in his being disinherited. He was firm in his choice, however, and in 1905 he entered the Presbyterian College in Tokyo, in preparation for the ministry. There he distinguished himself first as an ominvorous reader (his taste running to Kant, Darwin, Ruskin, and Max Müller) and second as a lover and defender of the weak and needy.

At the time of the Russo-Japanese War Kagawa, who had been deeply influenced by Tolstoi, declared himself a pacifist, and as a result one night was taken out to the baseball ground by his fellow-students and beaten. Years later, one of those whose blows had fallen upon him again laid hands upon him, this time to offer his ordination prayer!

While still in the second year of college he was stricken with tuberculosis, and had to seek health on the seashore, where he spent himself in the service of the fishing folk about him. It was there that he drafted his first novel which was one day to give him a foremost place among the writers of Japan. He wrote in such poverty that it had to be inscribed with the Japanese writing brush on the pages of cast-away magazines.

When only partially recovered he went to Kobe to enter the theological seminary, and while yet in his seminary studies he felt the call of the slums of the city, the worst, perhaps, in all the world. At that time there were in this section, known as the Shinkawa, some twenty thousand outcasts, paupers, criminals, beggars, prostitutes, and defectives, who lived like homeless dogs in human kennels of filth and vermin and disease. Policemen feared to visit this district unless they went in groups. Often a single house, not more than six feet square, would accommodate a family of five, or two families of nine to ten persons. A community kitchen, a water hydrant, and a common toilet of unspeakable filth often served the needs of a score of families. The district swarmed with scrofulous, undernourished children, and the infantile mortality often reached the staggering height of over 500 in 1000.

Kagawa's one room was about six feet square, without a bed, stove, table, or chair. One of the first applicants for his aid was a man covered from head to foot with blotches of contagious itch. Kagawa, feeling that this was the great test for him, received him and made him his bedfellow. In time, opening his little room indiscriminately to people with all manner of diseases, he himself contracted not only the itch but also a dreaded eye disease from which he has never recovered.

Here in his Shinkawa home Kagawa cared for the sick, washing their infected clothes with his own hands, and taught the more ambitious of the population, holding classes in reading and writing at an early hour before his students went out to work. Here he became the champion of babies and children who had been rented out to old women at so much per month by parents who did not want them, and who were slowly allowed to starve by their callous custodians. Even while still in theological seminary Kagawa adopted one such child to prevent its being starved to death, and through slow months, while still carrying on work in the seminary, nursed it back to life. He continued to live in his six-by-six room but as his duties increased he added another room which served as a dispensary and hospital.

After his first novel had been discovered one day by a publisher who called at his house in search of material for a magazine, it was published in book form and in a short time Kagawa's name was a household word over the Empire. Other books rapidly appeared, all of them eagerly devoured by the public.

While Kagawa was attending the theological seminary he came to know a "Miss Spring," a young woman who was a worker in a factory where he had preached. Under his influence she accepted Christ's way of life, and longed to give herself in the same hard, high service that was being performed by the one who had brought her the message. Two of the most beautiful poems of this book tell of the life partnership to which this friendship led.

In 1914 the way opened for Kagawa to study for two years in America. He spent this time in Princeton Theological Seminary, and in investigating social service institutions in this country. Lucrative positions were offered him on his return to Japan, but he refused them all and returned to his little room in the slums.

In the course of time he found himself involved not only in the problems of his immediate neighbors, but in social issues which affected the well-being of millions throughout Japan. In 1921 he led striking workers in a procession several miles long, demanding the recognition of their union and voicing their radical demand: "Laborers are personalities. They are not commodities to be bought and sold according to a scale of wages based on the market price." More than once Kagawa was arrested, at one time being beaten with a saber and dragged hatless and shoeless to the police station.

It was not the army of industrial workers alone, however, that called forth the creative sympathy of Kagawa. The majority of Japan's workers are farmers, and in a country smaller than the state of California, eighty-two per cent of which cannot be cultivated, with a population per arable square mile of 2,418, or the most overcrowded in the world, the life of the rural population is particularly hard. Forty-six per cent of them are tenant farmers, and Kagawa found that the struggle for existence was constantly driving many of these to the cities, to swell the population of the slums. He found that the sources of supply for public and private prostitution were these poverty-stricken rural villages. In 1931, in Kagawa's hut in the Shinkawa, the first true peasant union in Japan was organized, the first of a long series of undertakings on the part of Kagawa for the farmer-folk. In the course of the years these have included widespread peasants' co-operatives, the peasants' "gospel schools" at which religion is interpreted in terms of scientific farming and village improvement, and in magazines designed to promote the co-operative movement among the peasants, to which Kagawa has been the chief contributor.

Kagawa is a tireless advocate of the co-operatives as the next step in bringing about a socialized economy. He has built up a medical co-operative in Tokyo with its own hospital and some 6,000 members, and has been responsible for the organization of consumers' co-operatives in many of the large cities. In one of these, in Osaka, polished rice may be bought which has been grown by peasant co-operators and milled by the consumers' co-operative. Suits of clothing may be purchased at this store for about five yen (two dollars). In addition to this, the city settlements in Tokyo and Osaka, with their kindergartens, shelters for the destitute, co-operative pawn shops, and banks, are well known all over Japan.

While proclaiming himself a socialist, he has stood uncompromisingly against extreme tactics of violence and hatred, and at times has met the full force of attack from the extreme left as well as from the right. As a pacifist, committed to the elimination of the economic causes of war, Kagawa organized the National Anti-War League in Japan in 1928. He has voiced his opposition to the imperialist policy of the government since 1931, and on a recent visit to China has taken occasion publicly to apologize for the conduct of his countrymen. As the leading spirit back of the Kingdom of God Movement he has been instrumental in uniting Christian forces of Japan in a campaign that has as its goal one million Christians in Japan, and the realization of love in social life.

While engaged in his manifold activities of speaking and directing the work of numerous social organizations in Japan Kagawa continues to be a prolific writer.

Kagawa now lives in a small village outside of Tokyo, but the demands of his enterprises all over the Japanese Empire, and urgent calls for his counsel and message in other parts of the world, have forced him to spend a large part of his time in travel. His health is still poor, yet he continues to turn out the work of several men, seemingly having found some hidden source of energy. Above all, he remains a man whose life is organized about prayer, having adopted the practice of spending a full hour in the early morning in fellowship with God.

COLOPHON

SONGS FROM THE SLUMS *was composed on the Monotype in twelve point Garamond, leaded one point. Little is known of Claud Garamond, the individual, except the fact that he was conceded by his contemporaries to be the most famous type designer of his time (1541). Garamond has vivified his type by introducing a decided contrast in the main and minor lines, and freedom in curves. The long ascenders and descenders not only enhance the beauty and gracefulness of the letters, but make reading easy and prevent the frequent error of crowding the lines.*

The body of the book is printed on eighty-pound Beckett Offset; end sheets are seventy-pound Twilmark Text, and case is of Saylcom cloth stamped in gold Brighten Leaf.

DESIGNED BY
A. E. DISTELHURST
SET UP, ELECTROPLATED, PRINTED,
AND BOUND BY
THE PARTHENON PRESS
NASHVILLE, TENNESSEE